Dirt Farmer's Daughter

Dirt Farmer's Daughter

From a Dirt Farmer's Daughter to a Successful Woman

Daisy (West) DuBose

Strategic Book Publishing and Rights Co.

Strategic Book Publishing and Rights Co., LLC
USA | Singapore
www.sbpra.net

For information about special discounts for bulk purchases, please contact Strategic Book Publishing and Rights Co. Special Sales at bookorder@sbpra.net.

ISBN: 978-1-68235-399-8

Index

Introduction

When I was a child, my dreams were simple. I wanted a devoted husband that loved God, four children (two girls and two boys. I wanted a house with bedrooms for all of us, a white picket fence and a fire place. The teacher and pastor positions were the only professional positions that I grow-up knowing about. Therefore, I was undecided if I wanted to be a pastor or a teacher. But I was more persuaded to becoming a teacher instead of a pastor. This was because written in the Old Testament is a verse that say in church the wife should speak through her husband. If I was not sure about anything else, I was sure that I wanted to serve God.

My first year in grade school the teacher was very short patient with the children. It was the first time for some of the children to be apart from their mother and their home. They were frightened and confused. The teacher expressed little or no empathy for the children. Upon observing this first-grade teacher, I decided I wanted to be a teacher with a heart and understanding.

In the home in which I grew up there was no talk of what I want to become when I grow up. There were no program or examples to read about, no television and the only books in the house were school text books, the bible and the Sunday school book.

During my life time with God leading me and determination, I have developed through many stages. From a dirty farmers daughter, a maid/baby sitter, a kitchen helper in a hospital, shirt presser in a dry cleaner, a Cashier at a grocery store, a Clerk typist in Department of Commerce, a realtor, a purchasing agent in Department of Defense, a Contract Specialist in several Federal Government agencies, a Contracting Officer with the monetary authority warrant to obligate $100,000,000.00 of Tax payer's money with the US Army Corp of Engineers. I was an Award Fee Board Coordinator. In some of those positions I have instructed/tough others in acquisitions how to successful perform the duties of a Contract Specialist. In some cases, I have been the only African American in class rooms during the development of my education. I have been a pregnant teenager that struggled to feed and care for her children. Most difficult of all I have bought groceries, paid utility bills, paid rent, bought clothes for my three children with the $100.00 check that I received from Social Services each month. The trip to success was not easy. One day there was no bread in the house. I was short five cent from having enough money to buy a loaf of bread. I started the walk to the store as I walked, I prayed that God would let me find five cents on the ground before I got to the store. I walked, looking down on the ground, praying just before reaching the store there waiting on the ground was five cents. I thank God and proudly entered the store and bought the loaf of bread, took it home and feed my children.

I built my life through prayers and adapting good tracts that I saw in others. Through the years, I realized that it was me that had to love me. It was me that had to build for myself the life that I wanted to live. I love my mother dearly, but what she told me about finding a good man and he would take care of me did not turnout to be the plan best for me. I married four times and each husband was not husband material.

So, at 55 years of age, I setout to accomplished all the things that I dreamed of accomplishing with no husband by myside. I bought a house, and had a fire place built. Why the contractor was building the fire place I was siting across the room, looking at him with a smile on my face. He asked me why I was smiling. I told him that I had been married four times waiting for just one of my husbands to buy me a house with a fire place. Now, I was having it built for myself.

Followed after this, I reluctantly stepped out into the world with a lost sense of direction and with God as my guide. I have had jobs that paid me a 6-figure salary. There were times in my travel, I would get lost. At those times I would pray and God would put someone in my present to point me in the right direct.

Acknowledgment

For their encouragement and advice in assembling mush of the material upon which this book is based, I would like to express my sincere appreciation to my Granddaughter, Thia Beard, my late friend Gloria, my son Robert.

To my sister Mae and Son, Robert for them continuing to push me to write this book.

I especially want to thank my son Robert for locating a publisher to publish my bibliography.

I thank the rest of my children for being the best that they can be. I am proud of their accomplishments.

Last but not least, I want to thank my Philippines friends, that welcomed me into their circle. They called me Mom-D.

The views expressed in this book are my own, and for them I accept full responsibility.

Chapter 1

From Where I Came

I came from a family that made a living from digging in someone else's dirt. My mother and daddy were two hard-working people. They shared the same vision when it came to a safe home, filled with love, laughter, and all the things that made life comfortable. They worked as sharecroppers from sunup until sundown, digging in the dirt and watching plants grow.

We planted and grew peanuts, corn, and cotton. After all our hard work, at harvest time, when the crops were sold, a major part of the profit was giving to the landowner. My daddy received enough cash to give us a conformable life, buy seeds for the next year, and to keep us safe and warm through the winter. There was no way, or thoughts, that daddy would ever get rich or owner his own land and house. We were just underpaid servants working on the white man's land.

The landowner also owned the grocery store. It was the only grocery story in the small town of Seven, North Carolina. Therefore, part of the money Daddy made from working the farms was paid back to the landowner at the grocery store. Daddy would only buy groceries that he could not grow in the garden or meats he could not raise or hunt and kill. He went hunting for rabbits and squirrels and caught fish from the lake. We raised chickens, ducks, hogs, and geese. This gave us a verity of meats to eat. The flour to make bread was brought from the grocery store. It was packed in a cloth flowered bag. Mom used that bag to make my two sisters and I dresses and blouses.

Once a year Daddy had hog-slaughtering day. He would kill the fatty hog, cut him up, and preserve the meat in the smokehouse packed in salt. We did not have a refrigerator or a freezer. For dessert, we gathered berries and grapes from the woods, and peaches, apples, and pears from the trees in the yard. Mom would make jelly, jam, and preserves, and store them in glass jars. She made enough of these desserts in the summer to last all year.

Until I was nine years old, we did not have electricity. We did not have faucet water until I was twelve years old. Our water came from a well located in the front yard. Our lights came from oil lamps that sit on the table.

We were happy. There was a lot of laughter, sharing, and love in the home that they built for us. My parents never argued about anything. I guess it was because she was 5' 2" and weighed only 98 pounds and he was 6' 3" and weighed 210 pounds. Or maybe it was because they really loved each other.

Daddy only had a first-grade education. But he was a resilient man. He could build buildings, repair cars, trucks, tractors, and find legal ways to earn money to take care of his family. In addition to his farm work and raising farm animals, Daddy learned how to gather iron and sell it to make extra money.

When he came home from his iron-selling trips, he would call me and my brother into the sitting room and throw money on the floor to see which one of us could pick up the most money. The other game Daddy like to see us play was, me and my brother wrenching," because my brother was weak and I could beat him. Later my brother became stronger than me; that's when the wrenching game stopped.

With plenty of food in the house and clothes my mother made, we wanted for nothing. There was never a day that we went hungry. Our home was large enough so that we all had separate bedrooms. We considered ourselves a middle-class family.

Our furniture was nice, and our home was always clean. There were none of the modem appliances, no air conditioning, bathtub, or shower. We bathed in a wash pan and washed our clothes in a tin tub. We brushed our teeth with soda or soap and used a stick from a special tree for a toothbrush. Our food was fried in lard that came from the fat of the hogs on hog slaughtering day. This hog fat was also used to make soap for washing clothes.

Each Sunday morning, we would get dressed and ride to church sitting in the back of a wagon pulled by one mule. Mom and Daddy would sit on the bench at the front of the wagon and we would sit on the floor in the back. The sweat smell of spring flowers filled the air around us. The mules hoof clucking against the ground and mother humming a song throughout the trip to church made the ride very pleasant and field with laughter and love.

As a child being happily born and raised in the country where we had no television and where we could not go to a movie, and only allowed to listen to gospel music on the radio there was not many role-models to choice from. Therefore, I looked up to the only role models that I knew. That was country women with beautiful dresses, wide-brimmed hats, and high-heel shoes. These ladies appeared to be happily married and their children were well mannered. Therefore, my dream was to marry a farmer, have four children, raise chickens, go to church each Sunday, and live in a house with a white picket fence. At twelve years old, I ordered a hairbrush set. I said I was going to keep it to fix my little girl's hair and watch her run to get on the bus for school "each morning".

Chapter 2

The Change

Then one evening Daddy called us in to his bedroom. He asked my sister, my brother, and me to sit down. He wanted to talk to us. He asked us if we were tired of farming. Each of us said yes. Then he asked if we wanted to move to the city. This was exciting to us. We had never seen a city. A town with one grocery store, and a five and dime store was the largest commercial place that we had ever saw. We visited the town only when Daddy bought groceries at the landowner's store. After we said yes, he told us that on the next morning he was leaving to go to Norfolk, Virginia, locate a house, and get a job. Then after that, he would come back to get us. We were so happy to know that we would no longer be required to get up at the break of daylight and work in the field before catching the bus to school.

At age fifteen we moved to the large city of Norfolk, VA. It was the largest city I had ever seen. The house that daddy rented was furnished. He told mother to leave everything behind except our clothes and the kitchenware. Mother never questioned Daddy. She believed in him and trusted he would take care of us. We left behind everything we owned (furniture, farming tools, pictures on the wall, curtains, and rugs, if you can name it, we left it all behind). This felt like the happiest day of my life.

We got into the truck, looking like the Beverly Hillbillies. Daddy headed for our new home in the big city. After hours of driving, he arrived in front of this big, beautiful, white two-story house, situated on a comer lot. There were other houses located within voice range distance apart. The house we lived in, in the county was five miles from the neighbor's house. When we saw the new house, our excitement intensified. Living next door to another family was all new and exciting for us.

We jumped out of the truck and started running toward the house when Daddy stopped us in our tracks. He said, "Wait, Wait. We do not have the full house. He went on to explain that he had rented only the downstairs part of the house. This was another first for us. The first time we shared a house with another family. Little did I know, our life of plenty, living in the Garden of Eden had drastically changed. There was more first to come.

Daddy opened the door and we entered. There was only one bedroom, a living room, a kitchen, and a bathroom. There were five of us. We asked Daddy where were we suppose to sleep. He replied, "Here in the living room." He replaced the living room furniture with a double bed and a single bed and put up a curtain to separate the living room from the one bedroom. It was different. There was no privacy. Mother said, "Do not complain, children your daddy did the best he could."

Mother went back to Seven, NC to work in the peanut factory. She said it was so we could have more money. Daddy worked in a construction company in Norfolk near the house. While Mother was working away from home, Daddy did not buy any food for us to eat. This was the first time in our life that we experienced hunger pains. With the last bit of flour and grease in the house my sister made some gravy. With this being the last food in the house my sixteen-year-old brother went walking and asking store owners for a job so he could buy food for us. He told a store owner about our condition, and the man gave him a job along with some aged meat to bring to us to eat. From that day, he provided food until Mom came back home to live.

During this time, I was no longer enrolled in school. This was because there was no one to enroll me into school. For 4-months I did not go to school. Dad said, I did not need to go to school, that school was a waste of time. But I wanted to go to school, because I had dreams of a better life. Although, being a country girl was all that I knew, and I did not have any idea on how to obtain a better way of living, but I knew that it was out there somewhere.

Finally, my oldest sister enrolled me in the ninth grade at Jay Cox Jr. School in Norfolk. It was a 45-minute walk from the house to school. Rain, wind, or snow, I walked each day. I was happy to be in school again. Even-through I was only in the ninth grade, I had my eyes on entering the college doors. Upon completion of ninth grade, I would have been in high school, emerging into a woman and becoming my own person. This dream was cut short.

My time at Jay Cox Jr. School was confusing. I tried to fit-in, but I did not know where I fit. It was a school for black people only. But there was segregation even within the black race. During recess, the kids would gather into groups. The extremely light-skinned girls would be together, the tan-skinned girls would be in another group, and the heavily dark-skinned girls were in the third group. Being born and raised in a family that included all those complexions, I did not know which group I should join, and no group tried to befriend me. So, at recess I would sit alone and walk home alone from school. I was okay with this because I had my eyes on the bigger picture. Then one day, out of nowhere my dreams were shattered by a group of boys.

One day as I was walking home from school, a group of boys noticed me walking alone and begin to throw rocks at me each day. This happened many times after that. I would run as fast as I could, trying not to get hurt. After two days of running, I told my mother about the danger I was in. She just told me that I had to learn how to get along with the school kids. I guess she had enough on her plate, working away from home trying to help support us. I was left feeling that there was no one to help me to stay safe. Then and there, I made the decision to drop out of school.

Now, I was stuck in the house without a vision of a better future. It seemed like my dreams of prom night and entering college were buried under a pile of emptiness. How could I, at fifteen, figure out how to fix this so I could reenter school without getting hurt or killed? I did not have money for any type of transportation. There was no one to drive me to school, and Daddy thought school was a waste of time. To add to this wall of emptiness, my mother stuck me with providing free babysitting service for my oldest sister's kids. I asked myself, is this what I was born to do? I became very frustrated. This feeling brought me to speak to my mother disrespectfully, I told her if I wanted to babysit children as a life career, I would have my own.

Chapter 3

Spoken into Existence

Watch what you profess from your lips, because it will become a fact of life. Living a restless, meaningless life as a teenager, I began to go out at night to my neighbor's house. This house was two houses down the street from the house where we lived. The home owner was in her twenties. She always had a lot of people, men and women, at her house. They would be drinking, eating, dancing, and having a good time. One night I met and slept with a man who became my first child's father. It was not too long after that, at about 15, I became pregnant. When Mother learned that I was with child she put me on a bus to New York to live with my sister and told me not to come back until I gave away my baby. Giving away my baby was not acceptable. My baby would be the first person in my life that would really love, want and depend on me.

I got onboard the bus. This was my first time on a bus. I was afraid out of my mind. The Greyhound bus drove by our house. I saw my mother standing in the yard. With tears in my eyes, I waved, not knowing what lay ahead or if I would every return or get a chance to finish my education. After many miles of riding toward New York the bus stopped for gas. Remembering a story my father told us about when he traveled to Chicago to visit his mother it made me afraid to get off the bus to buy food. During my father's travel to visit his mother, he got off the bus to buy food and the bus driver drove away without him. He did not know where he was and had to learn how to get back home. He never tried to visit his mother again. I thought, if this happen to me, what would I do. I did not have enough money to buy another ticket, and I only had a one-way ticket to New York.

By the time the bus reached the second stop, I was so hungry, I had no choice but to take a chance, get off the bus, and buy food. I was so nervous; I dropped the silverware. Everyone in the bus stop stared at me. I do not remember buying any food. I ran back to the bus and stayed on it through the duration of the trip. Happily, my sister was waiting for me at Grand Central Station in New York City. We went to her apartment. There I stayed until my baby boy was born.

My son was born three months after my sixteenth birthday. He was 7 lbs. 5 oz. He was born on July 18, 1961. He was small and needed me to care for him. I was struggling to heal from his birth with breast pain caused by an abundance of milk that was blocked in my breast. The milk was blocked by a tumor that had been growing in my breast since they started to develop. One night while I was asleep, the right breast busted. The next day my sister took me to the hospital where she worked. She left me in the emergency room because she had to start her tour of duty. Being a 16-year-old girl, I did not know what to expect. Two nurses that attended to me, without pain killed, sat me in a chair one nurse while held my shoulder. The second nurse took a pair of scissors and cut my breast to insert a tube for drainage. After they inserted the tube, they sent me back to my sister's apartment. My condition was not improving, so, I returned to Mom and Dad in Norfolk. There my daddy put me into the hospital where the knot was removed from my breast, after which I began to heal. Now, I was determined on finding a father for my son and a lifetime husband.

After I recovered, I got a job as a nanny/maid to earn money to support my son and me. This job kept me away from my son five nights a week. He was left in the care of my mother. It paid $25 a week. I was not pleased with the care of my son. One weekend I came home, and my son was in the crib, wet and crying. No one was looking after him. So, I quit that job and searched for another one. My second job was at Norfolk General Hospital. This job paid $30 a week for a kitchen assistant. At Norfolk General Hospital. I met a handsome young man named James who worked at the hospital. As a floor buffer/polisher. It was not long after we met that I became pregnant with my second child. We got married and moved in with my parents. Now I had the perfect family-a man named James and pregnant with my second child. Life was wonderful, so I thought. I was happy. This marriage did not last long before my husband began to beat me for no apparent reasons. These beatings led to a divorce within four years after marriage.

Chapter 4

Life Lessons

There are many roads of life a person must travel during one lifetime. These roads build character, personality, temperament, and strength. When choosing these roads of life, it is important that you choose carefully, stay focused, and have a desire, a vision, and a goal. Let the vision include the comfort you want to enjoy in your life. There are no maps to follow, no short cuts or fast routes, but there are smart cuts. You just have to pray and trust God to guide you, be able to recognize the smart cuts and turn around if you have selected the wrong road.

As a country girl, growing up, I did not know much about life. I was surrounded by women who got married, had children, and worked in the fields beside their husbands. All I was sure of was that I wanted to go to college, marry a man named James, have four children, and live in a big house with a white picket fence and a fireplace. I wanted my husband and family to be active in church and love the Lord their God with all their heart.

Growing up, I do not remember my parents trying to teach me how to be successful in a career or life, nor did they teach me how to be a good wife. But they did teach me how to recognize value. This was because all they knew was the life they were living. How to accomplish my goals, were behaviors that I had to learn on my own. Norfolk provided another view on life. There were people with different job skills and different educational skills. I studied them and picked out the good parts and built myself with the help of God.

My lesson in romance came when I was sent to live in New York with my sister. My sister started buying *True Romance* comic books, which gave a false view of romance. As I look back, I wish there had been someone to help me prepare for the future, to help guide me in a direction where I could have avoided some of the hard roads that I entered. I thank God that he turned me around before my soul got lost in the dark place of no return, liquor, drugs, and prostitution. God guided me, placed people in my life that took interest in my development.

With one failed marriage, I kept trying and failing in marriage. I was still determined to find a father for my sons and a lifetime husband. I was under the misconception that the man that choose me to be his wife, that he would love my children as much as I. I discovered through several relationships; they were more resentful than loving toward my children. James, my first husband would stand Steven against the wall and beat him because he was late learning to walk. At the city park Edgar would put Cynthia in the tree and call her a monkey. Jesse tried to hurt Steven when they were playing wrenching in the yard. Steven had to wear a cast on his arm for weeks. It was not until after my fourth child and my third marriage that my focus returned to education.

Chapter 5

Against All Odds

After so many years of not reading, I had lost the ability to read. I enrolled in night school. I expected learning would be difficult but I was not prepared for the embarrassment that I received. One night the teacher asked me to read in front of the class. I politely explained to her that I was not confrontable reading in front of the class. Without considering my feeling, in front of the class, she said, I can't teach anyone that cannot read, you are in the wrong class. All the students laughed. I dropped out of night school. However, I still had my restless desires and a yearning for a better life for myself and my children, and I knew I had to find a way to succeed. Through three failed marriages, I had now learned that my happiness did not reside in the arms of a man. I had to find my own success. Highly determined and motivated, my search continued. Through talking to people, I learned about the GED test. I knew that I did not have the reading skills or the testing skills to pass the GED exam. However, this was the stumbling block that I had to conquer to make a major change in my life for myself and my children. So, I went to work on getting my GED.

After obtaining my GED, I took the diploma, and drove to Tidewater Community College, and sat down with a counselor. In the interview the counselor asked me what I wanted to be. I told him I did not know. But what I did know was that I did not want to be what I am. The counselor smiled and opened the college catalog and began to read different curriculums. When he reached the Associate Degree for Executive Secretarial Science, I said, "That is the one." That day, I enrolled in college, and purchased my books for class and a dictionary.

When I reached home, I opened the books and stared at the words on the pages. I prayed to God, in Jesus' name, asking him to open my mind so, I could read the words in these books, retain and be able to recall what I learned in order to pass the test that would be presented to me. There were times when I was up all-night studying. I had to look up words in the dictionary to learn how to pronounce them, learn their meaning, and how to spell them. It was difficult. But I learned through my parents' teaching that with God all things are possible. It was not up to me, nor was it done through my abilities.

It was God because, as He said, put him first in your life, and He will open doors that you never dreamed was possible. I remember one night as I was struggling to read, I prayed to God, I ask him to open my mind so I could learn to read or take my sight because my sight was no good to me if I could not read. I prayed that it was up to him whether he open my mind or removed my sight. He opened my mind; and one glorious day I walked across the stage and was handed my Associate of Applied Science Degree in Executive Secretary Science. My three children and my mother were setting in the bleachers, and my children yelled, "That's my mom!" There was no prouder minute than the minute I heard my children's voice and the dean handed me my college degree.

During this time, my life continued to evolve. I was in my third marriage. This husband was a cheater and a wife-beater. On the day of the graduation, he had beat me so badly the night before, I was limping across the stage when I got my degree. My mother was not aware of the pain in my body from the beating. Shortly after graduation my marriage ended.

Before graduation I was working in a grocery story as a cashier. After I graduated, I was hired into my second professional job. It was at Norfolk Shipbuilding and Drydock. My first position was a Payroll Clerk, then I was promoted to Accounts Payable Technician. This career came with a $10,000 bonus after ten years of service and paid a salary of $39,950 per year. I left that employment after nine years to marry my fourth husband and move to Cincinnati, Ohio. Left behind was my two older sons. They stayed in an apartment in Norfolk, VA. My two daughters moved with me to Ohio. Cynthia was in high school and Jessica was in grade school. In Ohio I gave birth to my fifth child, a boy. After my child was born, my husband and I moved to Maryland.

However, there was still that yearning in me to do more, learn more, and get a higher degree. Finding a college or university that would accept me was not easy, because I graduated from TCC with a 2.6 GPA. After much research, I located a college, what was later renamed National Louis University. I enrolled in National Louis University and earned my Bachelor of Science in Business Administration. With this degree my GPA was 2.9, which was not much better.

Still, I was satisfied with my education. The Bachelor degree was beneficial and help start my career in the Federal Government as a Clerk Typist GS3. I was earning promotions on my job. My career had excelled, and I rose to a GS9 position as a Purchasing Agent. At this level, my co-workers were attending acquisition classes. As a Clerk Typist I was not eligible to take those classes. To learn the duties of the Contract Specialist and a Contracting Officer, I would borrow their textbooks, copy them, and study the material during lunchbreak and evening when I was at home. This is how I learned to be successful in interviews for a GS11 position in the Federal Government?

I was not interested is earning a Master's degree until I was hired as a GS11 Contract Administrator with Defense Contracting Management Agency (DCMA) in Baltimore. My boss kept insisting that I return to college and earn my Masters. He said, without the Master's degree I would be stuck in my career.

Listening to him, I enrolled in Phoenix University, which was basically online. These courses were expensive. My job only paid 10 per cent of the cost. Also, because I had graduated with a 2.9 with my bachelor's degree, it was a requirement that I keep a 3.5 GPA average for the first three subjects to stay enrolled in the university. I was keeping a 3.5 GPA until my job sent me to Norfolk to take a mandatory quantitative Math course that I had to have to keep my job.

During the two weeks that I was in Norfolk taking the quantitative Math course, I did not have access to a computer. This caused me to lose my 3.5 GPA. When that happened, I was dropped from the university and banned from enrolling in any other university for two years. In the meantime, I kept praying for God to open a way for me to return to college without cost from my packet. Because financially, I was struggling to pay mortgage payments, feed and cloth three children and to keep transportation to get two and from work.

Then one day God heard my pray and open the doors of heaven. Setting at my desk in Baltimore, MD, working for DCMA, I received a telephone call from a Lieutenant Colonel (LTC). This LTC was stationed in Maryland and worked at NAVSEA. In the call he asked me if I wanted to work at NAVSEA. He explained that NAVSEA was located in Indian Head, Maryland and asked if I was familiar with the location. I answer by saying, yes, my house is 20 minutes from the base. The position was advertised as a GS 12. He asked me if I was willing accept the position as a GS 11 Contract Specialist. Before accepting the position, I ask if he was willing to sign an agreement that after 12-months of service, and proving that I was more than capable of performing the duties of the position that I would be promoted to a GS 12 without competition. The LTC signed the agreement and I went to work at NAVSEA as a Contract Specialist. My duties there were to administer Government contracts. To assure goods and services were received in according with the terms and conditions written in the contract. To assure the goods and services were accepted by the Government and all Government furnished equipment was returned to the Government and all Patent requirements were satisfied. After that to assure the contractor had been paid in full in a timely matter. I worked diligently and performed the duties with accuracy. At the end of twelve months, I was promoted to a GS12. In the meantime, God was still working in the background. He remembered my prays for a higher education without cost to me. This came through the Naval Seas Systems Command (NAVSEA) position that I had accepted. Within weeks after accepting the position, an announcement came out that for any employee who wanted to further their education, NAVSEA would cover the total cost. I enrolled in Central Michigan University and earned my Master's degree in Business Administration. By this time, I had learned the importance of a GPA. I aimed for a 4.0 and earned a 3.56 GPA. I had reached for the stars and landed happily on the moon. This made me proud to have God on my side for making these accomplishments possible and for the position in life where I had come from to the direction my life was headed.

Chapter 6

Unthought of Places

My God and my life hunger have taken me to places I never thought of traveling to, and never dreamed of or knew existed. In positions I never dreamed was within my reach. I have worked in important leadership positions, tough classes, and assisted co-workers in performing the duties of their job. Soldiers and subordinances looked up to me to teach them in their careers. I have helped other be able to enroll in classes to excel in their career.

The month I graduated with my Master's in Business Administration, I received a call from a U.S Federal Government base in Asia. Support Group-Kuwait, Which offered me a Contract Specialist position overseas. Oh, how good God is. He helped me to developed from a sixteen-year-old girl that could not read, that was struggling to feed and support three children, graduated with a 3.56 GPA from a creditable university at no cost to me. Now, I was being offered a job in Kuwait. I had never heard of Kuwait. Not knowing its location in the world, I placed the lady on the phone on hold and went to the map that was hanging in the hallway of my building to search for Kuwait. Noticing that it was located extremely near Iraq. I was reluctant to accept the position because Kuwait was near Iraq. With the lady on the telephone on hold, I stopped by a coworker's desk to ask her opinion. She told me to talk to another co-worker who had just came from over that side of the world before giving the lady an answer. When I explained to the second coworker about the offer, he told me to tell the lady on the phone that I would accept the position and come back to him and we would talk.

Following his suggestion, I told the lady I would accept the position in Kuwait. The second co-worker explained to me that Kuwait was not in damage of the war in Iraq that I would be self. In the position in Kuwait, I held three titles simultaneously, a Contract Administrator, Award Fee Board Coordinator, and Contract Officer Representative (COR). I earned $235,000 per year and received a $25,000 sign-on bonus 45 days after accepting the position. This was much more than my earnings as a farmer's daughter, babysitter, store clerk, clerk typist, or contract specialist. I worked there for 13 months before NAVSEA pulled my security clearance and I had to return to my job at NAVSEA. They were upset because I had gone over their head and wrote to the Secretary of the Army to get NAVSEA to hold my job at NAVSEA while I was working in Kuwait. Two months after returning to my Contract Specialist position at NAVSEA, they restored my security clearance. They did not have any grounds to cancel my security clearance.

The position at NAVSEA was easy and secure but it was not challenging. I was a GS13 Contract Specialist, and that was as far as I was going to go. Nevertheless, I sat there day after day without a desire to leave again. However, my resume was on the website. One day, I received a call from Aberdeen Proving Ground in Maryland. This job offered me a down payment on a house, my own office, as a team lead. I went on the interview, but not because I wanted the job. It was because I had bought my first car with a GPS system, and I wanted to try it out to see how it worked. I arrived at the interview ten minutes late. Once I arrived and entered the office by taking an eye survey, I noticed that there were two ladies sitting in the room at a large table. I sat across from them. The first words from my lips were, "Can I please have a glass of water?" One of the ladies got up and got me some water. Then the interview started. After the interview was over, we shook hands and parted ways. Two weeks later my supervisor at NAVSEA called me into her office and asked me if l was leaving NAVSEA again. I was astonished. I ask her what she meant. She said she had just received a phone call from a lady in Aberdeen Proving Ground asking for a release date. I told her I went on the interview just to try out my GPS system, not having any intention of getting the jb

Once I returned to my desk, I thought about the total offer. GS13 with a step increase equal to $1,200 more pay per year, a change to own another piece of property where the Government would make the down payment and pay the closing cost, my own team and office. The position became more attractive. I called the lady and accepted the position. As I was processing out to take the position in Aberdeen Proving Ground, and looking for temporary housing, I received a call from Fort Belvoir, Virginia. This position was a GS13 and it was located within driving distance from my home in Fort Washington, Maryland. Having the choice between the two, I accepted the Fort Belvoir position and turned down the one in Aberdeen Proving Ground. At Fort Belvoir, I was Team lead Contract Specialist, with a pay of $95,000 per year. This position came with responsibilities but no authority. The procurement teams were against each other. There was no unity. One team member could not ask advice from another team that was working on a similar project. It was not a pleasant place to work.

Some people would call it luck, but I think that God stepped in. My phone rang again. It was a call from Iraq with a job offer in Iraq for $265,000 and a $25,000 sign-on bonus. This became my second position in Asia. My title was Contracting Officer. After six months in this position the President of the U.S. gave orders that we had to leave Iraq. We were given the opportunity to go home or go to Afghanistan. Just think, I was afraid to accept the position in Kuwait because it was too close to Iraq. Now that I was working in Iraq, I was given the opportunity to decide to work in Afghanistan or go home to Maryland. Although my job in Fort Belvoir was on hold waiting for me to return, I had made a commitment to myself to spend two years in Asia.

I elected to go to Afghanistan. In Afghanistan, my title was Contracting Officer, with a team of six Contract Specialists, earnings of $265,000 plus a Social Security check of $12,000 a year. I was in this position for three and a half years, and they were still asking me to extend. After three and a half years in Afghanistan, I submitted my retirement papers and returned to Fort Belvoir.

My retirement lasted two days before I decided retirement was not for me at this time so, I decided to rejoin the workforce. It was my decision in 2012 to return to work as a contractor for the next two years. My plan was to bank my retirement check and live off my earnings as a contractor for two years. I put my resume back on site and went back to work in the yard. Shortly after, I got a phone call from a man who offered me a position as a contract specialist/contractor with earnings of $95,000 a year this position was located in Washington,DC. I turned him down. Minutes later the phone rang again. When I answered it, the man on the line offered me a position that paid $130,000 a year. I accepted his position and returned to the workforce. I worked for GCC Technology for twelve months, at the end of which I was given a $5,000 bonus. The company gave the employees a Christmas party.

It is a known fact if you put God first in your life, have a desire, determination, and stay focused, you can accomplish your dreams. Along the way there will be hard times, and people who will belittle the efforts that you are putting forward. They will tell you that you are wasting your time. You will never amount to anything.

You are too dumb to learn. All types of negative forces will come your way. Then there is you yourself; you'll try to make yourself give up. I was one subject from completing my Master's degree when I began to feel burned out. I did not sign up for the next semester and the last class. This is when I began to pray harder and talk to myself. Through these procedures, after taking one semester off, I signed up and took my last class and earned my Master degree. God had removed all obstacle that was blocking my path. He opened my mind so I could read, He removed prerequisites algebra requirement, He gave me the ability to clip the statistics course through taking a clip test, and He led me to an agency that paid the full amount for my Masters. Now, it was time for me to step forward and finish the race.

When I walked across the stage, not knowing if any family member would be setting in the audience. This was a far different situation then the one that I dream. My plan was that my family, mother, sister and all my children would be there. I had plan to rent a limousine to take me to the graduation. On graduation week none of my family had showed interest in attending. There weren't any funds to rent a limousine. I drove myself to the graduation location, I dressed in my graduation gown in the dressing room alone with tears in my eyes as I watched the other families helping their graduators dress in their gown. When I walked across the stage, I noticed my younger son, his girlfriend and my granddaughter was siting in the audience. After obtaining my degree we set down at the table and eat together. I thank God for taking me through and for the 3.56 GPA.

My travel took me from a dirt farmer's daughter, through an illiterate teenage mother, a four times divorced woman, to woman a with an executive position and a Master degree in Business Administration. Growing up where my daddy would give me and my sister $5 a week to spend when he took us to town help me to appreciate the journey that brought me here. Each step was a growth of strength, trust, acceptance and endurance.

I have stood head-to-head with Colonels, Lieutenant Colonels, Majors, and Captains where I provided guidance in the acquisition field. I shook hands with the President of the United States. I earned certificates, awards, and promotions. I have given speeches, lectures, been Headed the Award Fee Board briefings.

My travels have taken me to Germany, Thailand, Afghanistan, Kuwait, Ireland, Iraq and back to Kuwait again. As a teenager, laying on the blanket at the city park, looking at my children play there wasn't any way of knowing these things were possible. Thank God I did not listen to those people that told me how dumb I was and how I would never amount to anything.

Chapter 7

Planning for the Retirement

As I grew nearer to full retirement age, my thoughts began to be on the number one places to retire. I knew that shoveling snow and cutting grass were not desirable for a 70- to 96-year-old woman, and there were no prospects of marriage. After calculating my finances, I decided that Florida is warm year-round, and does not have state tax or personal property tax. Based on this, I chose Florida for my retirement home. I went back to Afghanistan to Camp Leatherneck. I worked there for 9-months and saved $75,000.00. Upon my return to the United States, I located a house in Fort Pierce, Florida in a new subdivision. The house was built in 2009. It had one owner that were headed into foreclosure. I bought the house without meeting the realtor and without seeing the property. During the process of transferring ownership, I was at my son's wedding in Colorado Springs, CO. I had the house professionally inspected, signed the documents and FedEx them back to the Realtor. Once the wedding was over, I returned to Maryland. My granddaughter and I drove to Florida. When we entered the subdivision, we looked at each other before we turned the corner and she said, ok let us see what you have bought. We were pleasantly surprised. The house had been advertised as a one-story family home with three bedrooms and two full baths. The realtor had left the key to the house under the mat at the front door. We gather the key and enter the house. First, we saw the three bedrooms that were located on the left side of the house. There was a wall that ran down the center of the house. On the left side of the wall was the three bedrooms and one full bathroom. After leaving the living room area, on the right side of the wall was the kitchen, family room. Once we entered that part of the house, we noticed a closed door. We said, wonder what is behind that door. When we open the door we discovered the master-bedroom with a full bathroom. I had purchased a four-bedroom house in a gated community, with a guard, swimming pool, clubhouse for as little as $120,000.00.

Our first day there we spend the night at an ex-coworker's house that lived in the neighborhood. The next morning my granddaughter and I dressed for work. We were ready to paint, clean and do what ever it took to get the place ready to live in. Gloria's brother was a construction worker that renovated homes. Gloria called her brother he came over and priced the job. He said for $10,000.00 he would paint the house and laydown new carpet. He said the $10,000.00 only paid for his labor any supplies or parts needed would be an additional cost. He said, that the bathtubs needed to be replaced. Needless to say, I turned him down. My granddaughter and I went to Walmart purchased cleaning material. She scrabbed the tubs until they became white, while I cleaned the kitchen and the rest of the house. After two-days of cleaning we called in a painter, a refrigerator repairman, a plumber, tree cuter and a carpet installer. The painter was instructed to paint the bedrooms first as the paint was drying in the bedrooms the carpet was being installed. In the meantime, the refrigerator repairman worked on the refrigerator for two days and charged $900.00. The refrigerator never worked. At the end I had to buy a new refrigerator. The address the repairman had given me for his place of business was someone else private home. We had one week (7-days) to renovate the house, buy furniture and return to Maryland. In Maryland I was scheduled to start a new job in 8-days. Once the carpet was laid, I sent my granddaughter out to purchase furniture. Her instruction was to by cheep and sent pictures. In the meantime, I stayed at the house with the contractors (the plumber, refrigerator repairman, tree remover, painter and the carpet installer). She was excellent on following instructions. The pictures she sent looked nice. They were from a second-hand store. The next day before delivery, I had an opportunity to visit the store and see the furniture that she had paid for before it was removed from the floor and placed in the truck. The pictures that she sent to me; the furniture looked 100% better in the pictures then it did when I was face to face with it. I told the store owner, that I wanted a refund because I did not like the furniture. The store owner refused to refund my money. I was forced to go the Bank of America (BOA) and get BOA to cancel the sale and return my money to my account. After BOA returned my money, they went after the storeowner for their money. My early lesson learned about Florida contractors; they are not to be trusted.

I bought the Florida house in 2014. It had a monthly mortgage payment of $900.00 per month. My new job that I was to start in 8-days after leaving Camp Leatherneck, Afghanistan was with GCS of McLean, VA. GCS had a contract with DHS in Washington, DC. My first day on the job was in June 2014. I worked there until July 21, 2017. On this job, in the United States, I earned $165,000.00 per year. My job title was Contract Closeout Specialist. I worked two days in the office and teller worked four days. The job was sweet and it was a joy to work there. In July 2017 GCS was not awarded the follow-on contract and the new contractor did not select me. Therefore, I was let go.

However, from Jun 2014 – July 21, 2017, I was working and living in both houses (Maryland and Florida). The days when I teller worked, I teller worked from Florida and the two days that I was required to be in the office that night I sleep in Maryland. I had the best of two worlds. But I stay focus on my retirement plan, I paid off my Florida home in 2017. My Florida home is mortgage-free and completed furnished. The only expense associated with my home is groceries, utility and entertainment expense, yearly property tax, and property insurance. When the job ended in Washington, DC, I decided to live in Florida full time. I accepted a job in Temple, FL at a pay of $85,000.00 a year. I worked that job for less than 90-days before I quit. As I was preparing to move back to Maryland, I received a call for a job in Orlanda, FL. Needless to say, I was not ready to move back in my home in Maryland. I was ready for a new life in a difference location. Orlando was one-hour from my home Florida house. It was a straight drive down 95 headed north.

With receiving my retirement check and Social Security I decided to accept the job for $80,000.00 a year. The job was with a contractor that had a contract with the Navy. My title there was Supervisor of the Contract Specialist Division. The duties were easy, and the atmosphere was pleasant. However, I still had the credit cards and the expenses that I had accumulated when I was earning $165,000.00 per year. This made making ends meet a struggle.

After one year of working there the contract went up for renewal the new company wanted me to stay on with a $10,000.00 raise and a $5,000.00 sign on bonus. I turned it down and accepted a position in Kuwait in Oct 2018. My job title in Kuwait at Camp Arifjan is a Contract Specialist with a salary that is Federal Income tax free. The company supply me with an apartment overlooking the ocean, private SUV, free gas, a maid twice a week, and two bonuses a year. I work 12-hour days with two days off each week.

During my time working here, I have renovated the Maryland house, paid off my Bentley, Nissan and Carvette, Partly, renovated the North Carolina house paid $18,000.00 to a hospital for a blood clot operation that was necessary due to COVID 19 Johnson and Johnson vaccination.

Chapter 8

Impressive Culture

Through my journey I have experienced the culture of the Philippines. Enjoyed the taste of their food. Learned about their culture, experience their happiness. At a weekend Philippine gathering, I could not help from noticing their happiness, their joy was unscanned. Sitting there watching, I thought about their unfair treatment in the workforce, their low pay and how they are force to live as a group in small accommodations, how they had to leave their county just to earn money to help out their family back home. Yet, they are happy and share a tremendous amount of joy. I observed how the male spends his time cooking and the female cleans up the kitchen after everyone finish eating. I observed how they pray before each meal and how they all held hands and prayed that we all have a safe trip back to our apartments. As I watch, it came to mind the scripture in the bible. "Trust in the lord with all your heart and soul. In all your ways submit unto him, do not be anxious about your life, what you eat or what you will wear, is not life more than food or clothing. Look at the bird of the air; they neither sow nor reap, nor gather into barns, and yet your heavenly father feeds them, are you not more value than they." Their happiness surpassed my greatest expectation. I have known people that have much more, more opportunities, more money yet they are miserable. Some to the point of taking their own life.

God have blessed me tremendously, through my journey from a share, dirt farmer's daughter to an accomplished lady.

The End.

Review Requested:

We'd like to know if you enjoyed the book.
Please consider leaving a review on the platform from which you purchased the book.

CPSIA information can be obtained
at www.ICGtesting.com
Printed in the USA
LVHW032139161121
703501LV00006B/166

9 781682 353998